the end of the
question mark

First published in Great Britain in 2006 by
Profile Books Ltd
3a Exmouth House
Pine Street
Exmouth Market
London EC1R 0JH
www.profilebooks.com

A CIP catalogue record for this book is available
from the British Library.

ISBN-10: 1 86197 869 3
ISBN-13: 978 1 86197 869 1

Text design and typesetting by Sue Lamble

Printed and bound in Great Britain by Bookmarque Ltd,
Croydon, Surrey

contents

acknowledgements

The founders of AQA would like to thank SHOP, the communication agency, for coming up with the idea of 'The End of the Question Mark' and Adam Howling, whose illustrations have brought to life its varied and ghastly deaths. We would also like to thank our researchers, the heart and soul of AQA, for putting the 'wow' into AQA's answers 24 hours a day. And finally we want to say a huge thank you to the general public who've already texted over 3.5 million questions to AQA looking for advice, information or simply a smile.

foreword

They loiter at the end of sentences like grammatical hoodies, standing in the way of progress and making us unsure of the world. For that they deserve to die. Who are we talking about? The insipid little squiggle that is... THE QUESTION MARK.

This book serves as a memorial to 3.5 million of the little creeps that The Great British Public have lined up, and AQA have gunned down, over two years since April 2004.

Feeling homicidal? Put one out of its misery now by texting any question to 63336. Wait a minute or so, and you'll get your answer packed into just one single text message, written by an AQA human researcher rather than some soulless appliance. It only costs £1 and if your question is as good as some of the gems in this book, you'll join our glorious hall of fame next year. Happy hunting. Oh, and if anyone asks, you're in waste management.

bouncy balls, lee jun fan & macbeth

? who was sid vicious named after

Sid Vicious of The Sex Pistols took his name from band member Johnny Rotten's hamster, who had a reputation for biting people. Sid died from drugs at 21.

? at what note does big ben chime

Big Ben chimes at a slightly off-note E, due to a crack in the bell's body which affects its pitch. Made in 1858, Big Ben weighs over 13 tonnes.

? which james bond film was named after an advertising slogan

'Diamonds are Forever' (1971) is the 007 film named after the De Beers advertising slogan 'A Diamond is Forever'. De Beers are credited in the film.

? **why did paul mccartney grow a moustache during the recording of sergeant pepper**

During the recording of 'Sgt. Pepper's' Paul McCartney had an accident on a scooter and so grew a moustache to hide a cut on his upper lip.

? **what film in the last decade won all the oscars it was nominated for**

The 2004 film 'The Lord of the Rings: The Return of the King' was nominated for 11 Oscars and won all 11 without having a single nomination for its cast.

? **what was the first advert on channel 5**

The first advertisement shown on Channel 5 was for the perfume 'Chanel No 5'. Channel 5 launched on Easter Sunday, 30 March 1997 at 6pm.

? who is the richest female under 25 in the south west uk and where does she drink

Grammy award-winning singer Joss Stone is 18 and worth £5m. She lives in Ashill, Devon. The local pub is 'The Square & Compass' (01823 480467). Good luck.

? what was the smiths crisp song years ago with little potato heads in the advert

Smith's Crisps advert tune (sung to the tune of 'Bobby's Girl') – 'We want to be (bum bum) Smi-ith's crisps, we want to be (bum bum) Smi-ith's crisps'.

? who made a plea from prison for his wife 2 get rid of a football team

Nelson Mandela told wife Winnie to disband her bodyguards, Mandela United FC, in 1989, after their alleged involvement in the death of Stompie Moeketsi.

in the advert for sony were the bouncy balls real or computerised

The Sony Bravia 'Bouncing Balls' ad used no computer graphics. An entire block of San Francisco was closed off for the shoot, which used 250,000 balls.

who died with buddy holly in an aeroplane crash

The airplane crash which claimed the life of Buddy Holly also killed Ritchie Valens, J.P. 'Big Bopper' Richardson and the pilot, Roger Peterson.

what is the world's oldest music record company

EMI Music UK and Ireland is the oldest record company in the world, dating back to 1897. It is also the world's largest independent music company.

? what is elliot from e.t.' s real name, and what other films has he been in

Henry Jackson Thomas, Jr, played 10-year-old Elliot in 'E.T. the Extra-Terrestrial'. He has also played in 'Legends of the Fall' and 'Gangs of New York'.

? what language was the bible originally written in

The Old Testament was written in Hebrew (with some chapters of Ezra and Daniel in Aramaic). The Christian New Testament was written in Koine Greek.

? procession of people riding. nine letters

A nine letter word meaning a procession of people on horseback is 'cavalcade'. It is a 16th century word from Italian 'cavalcare' – 'to ride on horseback'.

? how are ian and janet tough better known

Ian and Janet Tough are better known as The Krankies. The Scottish couple made themselves successful in the 1970s and 1980s in cabaret and television.

? why is it unlucky to whistle in a theatre dressing room

Whistling is unlucky in the theatre because whistles were used by stage hands to signal the moving of scenery. So an errant whistle could be disastrous.

? when was maybe it's because i'm a londoner written

'Maybe It's Because I'm A Londoner' was composed by Hubert Gregg in 1944. He claimed that the song only took him 20 minutes to write.

❓ what are the top 5 best selling albums of all time

Top album sales: 1. Eagles – 'Greatest Hits'. 2. Michael Jackson – 'Thriller'. 3. Pink Floyd – 'The Wall'. 4. Led Zeppelin – 'Untitled'. 5. AC/DC: 'Back in Black'.

❓ has anyone actually seen elvis's dead body

Dr Eric Muirhead was a pathologist who helped perform the autopsy on Elvis's body, so he saw it, as did the police, and his family of course. Elvis was 42 when he died.

❓ in the usa what do they use to clean blood off motorways

There is an urban legend that police officers in the US carry Coca-Cola in their cars to clean blood from the roads after traffic accidents. It is false.

❓ what is the track and artist on the nhs immunisation advert

The track and artist from the NHS Immunisation advert is 'You and Me Song' from the Wannadies. The advert was titled 'Always You and Me'.

? who would win a fight between the chuckle brothers and robson & jerome

Robson & Jerome would try to destroy them with a horrific duet, but the Chuckle Brothers would win with a terrific one-two, 'to you, to me' killer joke.

? who was the first character on screen in the soap night and day

The first character on screen in the TV series 'Night And Day' was Jane Harper, played by Georgina Walker. The ITV series began in 2001.

? who invented the 5 day working week

Henry Ford invented the modern 5 day working week in 1926. He decided to close his factories on Saturdays, thinking this would help spur the economy.

? the game of dobbers is an indoor version of what outdoor game

'Dobbers' is an indoor version of 'quoits' (an excellent scrabble word!). It is designed to be a tabletop version and you throw hoops to score points.

? 0.35195 fluid ounces is the cryptic clue i have to find the name of a band or singer and i'm stuck

The band or singer from the cryptic clue '0.35195 fl oz' is 10CC. The group got the name from the amount of semen the average male in the UK ejaculates.

? there is a painting i think it's called 'the slaying of the' it's by an artist i think dutch artist beginning with r. the image is king herod killing baby boys

The Bible story of the slaying of the innocents has been much painted over the centuries. The Dutch artist Rubens (1577–1640) is one of many to paint it.

? **who invented the magic eye puzzles that we used to know n love n how did they work**

Programmer Tom Baccei and artist Cheri Smith invented 'Magic Eye' stereograms in 1991. 'Magic Eye' works through depth perception by diverging both eyes.

? **how much did the famous painting of the sunflowers go for**

In March 1987 Yasuo Goto paid the equivalent of US $39,921,750 for Van Gogh's 'Sunflowers' painting. It is now in the Seiji Togo Yasuda Memorial Museum.

? **when was vodka first made**

Vodka is said to have been originally created from potatoes in Russia. The first documented production of vodka in Russia was at the end of the 9th century.

? where is the biggest mcdonald's in the world

The Moscow McDonald's is the largest in the world. The expansion of McDonald's Canada to Russia was accomplished after thirteen years and it cost $50m.

? why do northern soul dancers put talcum powder on the dance floor

The music is up-beat, so Northern Soul dancers put talcum powder on the floor to aid their dancing, which includes a lot of spins, twists and slides.

? who has won the most oscars

The actor with the most performance Oscars is Katharine Hepburn, winner of 4 statues. Walter Brennan, Ingrid Bergman and Jack Nicholson have 3 statues.

where is the maze that is in the film the shining

AQA hates to shatter an illusion, but the maze in 'The Shining' was built on sound stages at Elstree Film Studios, as were the hotel interiors.

who came 2nd in the people's face of '83 competition

Samantha Fox came second in the Sunday People's Face of '83 competition. AQA can only assume that the judges weren't really looking at her face.

where did harold shipman practise

In 1974, Dr Harold Shipman took his first GP position in Todmorden, west of Halifax, West Yorkshire, moving to the Donneybrook Medical Centre in Hyde in 1977.

? what is the meaning of stamping on a glass at the end of a jewish wedding ceremony

The act of breaking a glass is an expression of sadness at the destruction of the Temple in Jerusalem, and identifies the couple with the Jewish people.

? what should I do to my bird tonight

Different birds need different approaches. Prepared fowl need stuffing and basting, caged birds like a shared whistle, and real women like champagne and romance.

? where was duncan buried in macbeth

King Duncan (15 August 1001– 15 August, 1040) was buried at Iona, a small island of the Inner Hebrides in Scotland. Duncan was given the title 'The Gracious'.

? can you send me the lyrics
to 'teenage mutant hero
turtles'? only the bit
namechecking each turtle

> 'Leonardo leads, Donatello does
> machines (That's a fact, Jack),
> Raphael is cool but crude (Gimme a
> break), Michaelangelo is a party dude
> (Party)'.

? how old are the actresses that
play gail platt and audrey
roberts in coronation street

> Helen Worth, 55, plays Gail Platt in
> 'Coronation Street'. She was born on
> 7 January 1951. Sue Nicholls, 62,
> plays Audrey Roberts. She was born
> on 23 November 1943.

? what was the song playing
while john sim's character
was in the record shop
during last night's 'life on
mars' on bbc1

> The song playing in the record shop
> in 'Life On Mars' was 'Baba O'Riley' by
> the Who. The track appears on their
> 1971 album 'Who's Next'.

? when were the first ever flavoured crisps made and what flavour were they

Crisps were first made in the USA in 1853, and were just ready salted. The Tayto firm made the 1st flavoured crisps in 1953. They were cheese and onion.

? why are there 12 days of christmas

The 12 days are the period between Christmas & Epiphany which celebrates the visit of the Magi. It is unlucky to leave decorations up after this.

? on my coins i've just noticed that directly underneath the queen's neck are the tiny initials irb. it seems to me this started in '98. what does it stand for

The initials IRB on British currency coins stand for Ian Rank-Broadley. He is the artist responsible for the Queen's updated portrait.

? is mr t dead

> Happily, Mr T is still very much alive. In 2005 he announced he would never wear his chains again and donated a great deal to victims of Hurricane Katrina.

? number of questions a 4 yr old asks every day

> Although it may feel, at times, like an infinite number, AQA estimates that a 4 year old asks about 12 questions per waking hour – so around 150 per day.

? how many types of drugs did elvis have in his system when he died

> It is reported that 11 different drugs were found in Elvis Presley's system when he died; all were for medicinal purposes. He died on 16 August 1977.

? what does show us your jazz hands mean

> The term 'show us your jazz hands' requests the performer to raise both hands to head-height and wave them in an 'end of the minstrel show' way.

where does the word bar in relation to serving drinks come from

'Bar' can refer to the specialised counter on which the drinks are served and it's from this term that the establishment as a whole gets its name.

why do rabbis have long little finger nails

The Golem was part of Jewish folklore in the 16th century. This clay figure 'magically' grew fingernails to keep out evil; rabbis still grow their nails now.

why was the sundance kid called the sundance kid

The real name of the Sundance Kid was Harry Longabaugh. He got his nickname after stealing a horse in Sundance, Wyoming, and being sent to jail.

? who wrote the musical grease

Jim Jacobs and Warren Casey wrote the hit musical 'Grease.' Frankie Vallie wrote and sang the title song in the movie version.

? who sailed to sea in a sieve

The Jumblies, in a poem by Edward Lear, 'went to sea in a Sieve, they did, In a Sieve they went to sea, In spite of all their friends could say'.

? what is the most covered song by other artists of all time

The most covered song is 'Yesterday' by the Beatles. From 1965 to 1986, 1,600 versions were made and covered by artists including Elvis Presley and Gladys Knight.

? what is the most expensive taxi ride taken in the uk

The most expensive taxi ride taken from within the UK was from London to Cape Town (S. Africa) and back (21,691 miles). The £40,210 fare was waived.

? were any bugs bunny cartoons ever used as war propaganda

> Bugs was one of many cartoons used in WWII propaganda. He met Hermann Goering in 'Herr Meets Hare' and fought the Japanese in 'Bugs Bunny Nips the Nips'.

? who is the youngest nobel prize winner? how old was he? how old was andre gide when he won it

> The youngest person to receive a Nobel prize was Sir William Bragg, for Physics in 1915. He was 25 years old at the time. Gide was 78 when he won.

? name famous cartoon rabbits

> Bugs Bunny, Roger Rabbit, Rabbit (in Winnie), Bucky O'Hare, Buster Bunny, Babs Bunny, Lola, Thumper, Mr Whiskers and Bionic Bunny.

? what ford car did mad max use

> Mad Max's yellow interceptor car was a Ford Falcon XB sedan, with 351 V8 engine, probably a 1974 model. He is seen driving it before he goes mad.

? **did prince albert really have a pierced penis, ie. why are male genital piercings named after him**

Yes, Prince Albert did have a pierced penis. Legend has it he strapped his penis ring to the side of his leg in order to stop his trousers from bulging.

? **is the young girl who plays joanna in love actually really singing all i want for christmas is you, or is she pretending**

Olivia Olsen, who plays Joanna, did all her own singing in 'Love Actually'. She had such a good voice that it had to be edited to sound more child-like.

? **who was the first actor to be nominated for an oscar after he died**

James Dean was the first actor nominated for Best Actor after his death. He was nominated posthumously for 'East of Eden' and 'Giant'.

? who is the 3rd best selling author of all time

Agatha Christie is the world's 3rd best selling author of all time with 2 billion books sold in 44 languages. Beaten only by the Bible and Shakespeare.

? who played the villain in die hard the movie

In the first 'Die Hard' movie, Alan Rickman played Hans Gruber, the leader of the German terrorists. Planning is under way for a fourth 'Die Hard' film.

? what does the designation 007 mean

The Double-0 in 007 signifies that James Bond is licensed to kill by the British Secret Service. 7 is the number specifically designated to Bond.

? what is the smallest plane to fly transatlantic

The smallest plane to complete a transatlantic flight is the Laima. She made the flight unmanned, and weighed only 29lbs, flying UK-bound.

? what was the name of joy division before warsaw

Richard Boon and Pete Shelley from the Buzzcocks suggested the name Stiff Kittens but it didn't stick. They became Warsaw in 1977 and Joy Division in 1978.

? what connects montgomery clift, compton mackenzie and benjamin britten

Montgomery Clift, Compton Mackenzie and Benjamin Britten were all homosexual. Surveys suggest that around 7% of men have had homosexual sex.

? which rock and roll great pretended to be gay

> Jimi Hendrix pretended to be gay in order to be discharged from the army. He had previously claimed that he left in 1962 due to an injury.

? when did the first car drive on the streets of london

> The first car on the streets of London was in 1824 when English engineer Samuel Brown's adapted Newcomen engine burned gas and drove up Shooter's Hill.

? before die another day how many people did james bond kill on screen

> 1,183 have been killed by James Bond on screen, up until 2002's 'Die Another Day'. Roger Moore was the most lethal 007, with 586 dead.

who is arnold dorsey better known as

Arnold George Dorsey, born on 2 May 1936, in what was then known as Madras, India, is better known as Engelbert Humperdinck.

what is the longest time that a stuntman has been on fire, in a film, in a single shot

The world record for the longest full-body burn without oxygen is 2 minutes 38 seconds, set by the American stuntman Ted A. Batchelor on 17 July 2004.

what is bruce lee's real name in chinese

Bruce Lee's birth name was Lee Jun Fan in Cantonese, or Li Zhenfan in Mandarin. His name literally means 'invigorate San Francisco'. He died aged 32.

? in the disney film beauty & the beast, what was the name of the clock

The clock in the 1991 Disney film 'Beauty and the Beast' is called Cogsworth, voiced by David Ogden Stiers. In the French release he was called Big Ben.

? what does pink floyd mean

Pink Floyd got their name from the American blues artists Pink Ande and Floyd Council. Their last concert was on 2 July 2005 at Live 8.

? what brand of whisky does paulie throw at the rocky pinball machine in the film rocky 3

Paulie (played by Burt Young) throws a bottle of J&B Rare (Scottish whisky with a red and yellow label) at the Rocky pinball machine in 'Rocky 3' (1982).

? which american president's last words were i have a terrific headache

President Franklin D. Roosevelt famously said 'I have a terrific headache' before slumping at his desk and dying of a massive cerebral haemorrhage.

? what is widely considered to be the world's most valuable piece of recorded music

The most valuable record is 'That'll Be The Day', produced for 90p in 1958 by the Quarrymen (three of the Beatles), and recently purchased for £100,000.

? of all the songs to be at number one, which song had the longest duration

The Number One with the longest total running time is Oasis's 'All Around The World', which reached the top spot in 1998. It is 9 minutes 38 seconds long.

? why do people say bless you after we sneeze

We say 'bless you' after sneezing because in medieval times it was thought that sneezing expelled a person's soul.

? when did duck first start making tape

'Duck' tape (more commonly known as duct tape) was developed in 1942 for sealing WWII ammunition cases. After the war, it became popular in households.

? how old is madonna and when was her first single

Madonna is 49 years old. Her first single was 'Everybody' in 1982. It was not a pop hit, but it reached no.3 on the US Billboard Dance Chart.

? why do some 45 rpm records have big holes in the centre

The large hole in the centre of some 45 rpm records allows for easier handling by jukebox mechanisms. A 45 rpm single holds up to 6 minutes of audio per side.

? **what is the only oscar winning film that has no women speaking in it**

> 'Lawrence of Arabia' won seven Oscars in 1962 and featured no females in a speaking role. The only female in the entire film is a camel named Gladys.

? **why did lady penelope never get laid by any of the thunderbirds**

> Lady Penelope clearly thought there would be too many strings attached. Sleeping with the Thunderbirds can only lead to a complicated, tangled mess.

coats, taxis & condoms

? what people in britain are ineligible to vote

> The Queen, Peers of the Realm, felons
> and lunatics are not allowed to vote,
> which is a great weight off some
> people's minds.

? is it true that car drivers in paris are not insured for accidents on the road around the arc de triomphe

> It's true – drivers using the 10-lane
> Arc de Triomphe roundabout in Paris
> are not covered by their insurance.
> This is a notoriously dangerous road.

? how old do you have to be to drink in italy, canada, mexico, australia and new zealand

> Legal drinking ages – Italy, 16;
> Canada, 19 (18 in Alberta, Manitoba
> and Quebec); Mexico (rarely enforced)
> and Australia, 18; New Zealand, none
> (18 to buy).

? which actress wore the same coat in all her movies

Lassie was the 'actress' who always wore the same coat in all her movies. Lassie was created by the British-American author Eric Knight in 1938.

? which country uses the most condoms

Japan uses the most condoms in the world. 2.8 billion condoms are produced every year worldwide, and Japan uses 58% of them, or 1.624 billion.

? how long do you have to of died in order to be able to get a blue plaque outside where u lived

Blue Plaques: Under the main scheme, run by English Heritage, nominations are taken from the public for people who have been dead for at least 20 years.

? which city/town in england has the largest rat to human ratio

London has the highest rat to human ratio, with more rats (about 9 million) compared to 7 million humans. You're never more than 10 metres from a rat.

? in which village in england do they place a pig on a wall 2 watch the village fete

In the village of Gornal, West Midlands, there is a legend that a local put a pig on a wall to see a band go by. There's a pub called 'The Pig on the Wall'.

? where was the last manned lighthouse in the uk

The last manned lighthouse was in Fair Isle South, Shetland. It became automated in 1998. 1853 was the first time electric light was used in lighthouses.

? what is the name of the little silver diner next to the millet arms pub on the a40

The silver diner in Perivale near the Millet Arms on Western Avenue/the A40 is called Starvin' Marvin's Diner. The phone number is 020 8998 5132.

? how much profit do the country's speed cameras make in a day

With over 5,000 fixed speed cameras in England & Wales, the Government made £20m profit in 2005. That's £54,794 per day or £10.96 per camera each day.

? what are the royal towns of england

There are two Royal towns in England, Royal Tunbridge Wells in Kent and Royal Leamington Spa in Warwickshire. Berkshire is the only Royal county in England.

? how many people disappear every day in britain on average

It is estimated that 210,000 people go missing every year in Britain. This is on average about 575 people a day. Most of them return within a few days.

? what was the date and location of the first ever car theft

The first reported car theft occurred in St Louis in 1905, six years after the first recorded traffic fatality. Car alarms were invented in the 19th century.

? is big ben bigger than the statue of liberty

Big Ben is slightly bigger than the Statue of Liberty – 96.3m (316ft), and 93m (305ft) high respectively. Without its base, Liberty stands 46m (151ft).

how many taxis are there in britain

There are around 75,500 licensed taxi vehicles in the UK with 20,700 in London alone. There are almost twice as many licensed drivers as vehicles.

what is england's motto

The motto of England is 'Dieu et mon droit' (French for 'God and my right'). It was first used by Richard I in 1198 and was used as a motto under Henry VI.

why does the number 5 key on phones have 2 sticking out bits on either side

The no.5 button on a phone has bits sticking out on it to aid blind people. It lets them know where the 5 is, and they can work out the rest from there.

how much money does the royal family contribute to the uk economy

In 2005 income from the Royal estates amounted to £148m. However, this does not take all related tourism into account. Their expenditure was £35m.

? what % of the uk smoke

About 12 million adults in the UK smoke cigarettes, 28% of men and 24% of women. In 1974, 51% of men and 41% of women smoked cigarettes.

? which tube line is deeper, the piccadilly or the northern

The Northern Line is deeper than the Piccadilly Line. The Tube's deepest point below ground level is at Holly Bush Hill, Hampstead, 67.4m (221ft).

? which celebrities are from yorkshire

The Arctic Monkeys, Guy Fawkes, John Barry, Gareth Gates, Geoffrey Boycott, the Bronte sisters, Tony Christie and Jarvis Cocker are all from Yorkshire.

? how can i arrange dinner with the queen

The best way to have dinner with the Queen is to be elected leader of a foreign country and then be invited to Britain for an official visit. Good luck.

? how many koreans live in new malden, surrey

Since immigration restrictions were eased in 1989, Britain's Korean population has grown to about 30,000. Of those, about 20,000 live in New Malden.

? why does it say 562 on pint glasses

The number stamp on pint glasses refers to the authority that has checked the glass for size; it is called a Crown Stamp. The number 562 is from Bury.

? where is bin laden hiding

Recent reports suggest Osama Bin Laden is hiding in Chinese territory near the Pakistan border. He has allegedly made an agreement with local authorities.

? is it true that guinness tastes better in ireland than in the uk

Guinness tastes better in Ireland. It's travelled fewer miles, the publicans take great care storing it, and you can't beat Irish pubs for atmosphere.

? why, next to blackfriars bridge, are there columns not supporting anything

The empty red columns next to Blackfriars Bridge in London are all that remains of the old St Paul's Railway Bridge which was dismantled in 1984.

? what is the name for the dot on an i and where is the only place in britain that the queen can't visit

The dot on an i is called a tittle or tiddle. The Queen is not allowed into the House of Commons Chamber – the rule dates back to the reign of Charles I.

? **is castration a form of punishment for rape in any state in america**

> Yes, chemical castration is currently allowed by law in California, Florida, Montana, Texas and Georgia. It is used for serial sex offenders.

? **after the birth of george ray scott, population of britain rose to which figure**

> George Ray Scott was born a healthy 8lbs and 15oz and is normal apart from the fact that his birth means the UK population has reached 60 million.

? **what city in the world has the smallest population**

> There's no internationally agreed definition of 'city', but going by local definition the smallest city is St David's, Wales, population 2,000.

**? when did battersea power
station close down**

Battersea Power Station A closed in
1975 and Station B finally ended
production in 1983. It is a Grade II
listed building, and is being
redeveloped.

**? how would a person in the
uk contract liver fluke**

Sheep liver fluke (known as 'fasciola
hepatica') can be caught when you eat
contaminated vegetables. The most
common source is watercress.

**? what's the oldest pub in
london**

A few pubs lay claim to being the
'oldest pub in London'. The most
likely of these is Ye Olde Mitre on Ely
Place, EC1. It's said to have opened in
1546.

? how many fedex depots are there across the usa

Fedex has 1,450 offices, 321 service centres, 899 stations and 500 terminals in the USA. It has 260,000 employees and makes 6 million daily deliveries.

? where is it illegal to drive after eating garlic

It is illegal in Indiana to drive or attend a public theatre or cinema within four hours of eating garlic. It is also illegal to make a monkey smoke a fag.

? how many times does big ben strike in one day

The hour bell of Big Ben chimes 156 times a day, and the 4 quarter bells chime a collective total of 960 times a day. It chimes in the note of E.

how many people in the world have 11 toes

AQA estimates that about 6,483,600 people worldwide have 11 toes. About 1 in 500 babies has an extra finger or toe. The name for this is polydactyly.

how many people in the world have one blue eye and one green eye

60 million. One in 100 people have heterochromia, the condition of differently coloured eyes, including David Bowie, Kiefer Sutherland and Kate Bosworth.

can u spell llanfairporthgwingethgogeli ghwinrobollantasiliogochgo chgoch properly

Llanfairpwllgwyngyllgogerychwyrndr obwllllantysiliogogogoch is the correct spelling of the longest official place name in the UK. It's in Anglesey, Wales.

? where does the word chav come from

Chav is from a Geordie word 'charver', originally meaning 'slapper'. Chavs, also known as pikies and scallies, love designer labels, especially Burberry.

minty, liturgical & wuthering

how do you say rat in arabic

'Rat' in the Arabic language is 'jarth'.
In Dutch and French it is 'rat'; in
German it is 'Ratte'; in Italian it is
'ratto' and in Portuguese it is 'rato'.

what is paddywack

Paddywack is in fact dried, stretched,
smoked bullock penis. It is used as a
dog treat, hence the rhyme: 'Nick,
nack, paddywack, Give the dog a
bone'.

what's the history behind using the word honey as a show of affection

The word 'honey' as a term of
endearment goes back to 1350.
Shakespeare used it in 'Othello'.
Honey has always been associated
with good things.

why is a banana called a banana

The word 'banana' came via Spanish or Portuguese from an African language (possibly Wolof) in circa 1597. Bananas first appeared in written text in 600 BC.

people say things are dirty/ mucky or minty – where does the word minty come from

The word 'minty' is used in America and has been made famous by Seth Cohen in 'The O.C.'. The word refers to things of embarrassment and homosexuality.

where in the world could the windy man also known as the long mover be found

A 'windy man' or 'long mover' can be found in most reptile houses in zoos, the Amazon rainforest, and in glass tanks. The terms refer to a python.

? what word changes from the plural to the singular by adding an s

The word that changes from a plural to a singular by adding an 's' is 'princes'. By adding an 's' you turn more than one prince into one princess.

? who named the apple

The word 'apple' comes from the Old English word 'aeppel', used to refer to any round object. It is unknown who first used the word to describe the fruit.

? who invented toilet roll

Toilet roll was invented in China in AD 1391, when the Bureau of Imperial Supplies began making 720,000 sheets of toilet paper for Emperors every year.

? why is there a country called turkey and a bird called a turkey? is it a coincidence

> Turkeys are so called as they were associated with the turkey-cock bird which got its name from being imported through Turkey. It is not a coincidence.

? what does liturgical mean? well i know it comes from liturgy but what does that mean

> Liturgy: Worship of God through Christian sacrament. Liturgical: Of the church service. Coming from 'leitourgia', Greek for 'the work of the people'.

? why are peanuts called peanuts

> The peanut is so named as it is a species of the pea family, not a nut. After pollination, the developing fruit forces its way underground to mature.

what does wuthering mean

'Wuthering' is used to describe the wind, meaning to blow strongly and with a roaring sound. 'Wuthering Heights' was Emily Bronte's only novel.

what does honoroficabili-tudinitatibus mean

'Honoroficabilitudinitatibus' means honourableness – the quality of being honourable. It was the longest word used by Shakespeare (in 'Love's Labour's Lost').

what do you call a group of deer

A group of deer is called a 'herd' or 'mob'; male deer are called stags, harts, bucks or bulls. A baby deer is called a fawn and a female deer is a doe.

where does the word shandy come from

Shandy (shortened from Shandygaff) is thought to have originated in 17th century England and to have been named after a pub whose beer was off, so they sweetened it.

who invented the word cinnamon

The original name for 'cinnamon' came from the Malay word, kayumanis, meaning sweet wood. The Hebrew equivalent was qinnamon, the source of the word.

why are tetrapak cartons called that name

Tetrapak is so called because it is packaging that originally had 4 sides, and so was a tetrahedron. 'Tetra' means 4 in Greek. It was designed in 1950.

in slang when you use k to imply a thousand what does the k stand for

When the letter K is used to refer to 1,000, the K stands for 'Kip'. The name comes from combining the words 'kilo' and 'pound'.

? what is homiletics

Homiletics is the science that treats of the composition and delivery of a sermon or other religious discourse. It includes all forms of preaching.

? what does the word corollary mean

A corollary is a proposition that follows with little or no proof from one already proven. Simply put, it's a natural consequence or effect; a result.

? where does the saying come from cold enough 2 freeze the balls off a brass monkey and y are they called brass monkeys

Cannonballs were stored on ships on brass frames called 'monkeys'. If it was cold enough, the brass would contract hence letting the balls fall.

in london, the police are often known as jakes. where does the nickname originate and what does it mean

The nickname 'Jake' or 'Jakes' for police comes to London via the USA. It is derived from a TV show called 'Jake and the Fat Man' shown from 1987 to 1992.

what is predology the study of

Predology is the study of predators or 'Yautja'. The term is taken from the popular fictional 'Predator' films and mostly used by avid sci-fi fans.

what is the obsession of plutomania

Plutomania is an abnormal desire for wealth. A crush fetish is a paraphilia, which is the desire to see members of the opposite sex crush insects.

what is otoplasty

Otoplasty is the correct medical term for ear pinning. It is a type of cosmetic surgery. In Latin 'oto' means ear and 'plasty' means to change.

? what is the meaning of hotchpotch

'Hotchpotch' is used to mean odds and ends or an assortment of things. It is also the name of a thick soup made with beef, lamb, veal, vegetables and herbs.

? if i am sleeping with a polish lady what would be the best compliment i can pay them

In Polish, 'Lubie Cie' = 'I like you', 'Pragne Cie' = 'I want you' (desire) and 'Tesknie za Toba' = 'I miss you'. Also, 'Wygladasz super!' = 'you look hot'.

? bird name meaning idiot in portuguese

The dodo is the bird with a name close to 'doudo', the Portuguese word for an idiot. The name actually derives from 'dodors', Dutch for tail feathers.

what is a sket

'Sket' is a slang term meaning 'tramp', 'slut' or 'woman of ill-repute'. The term is a shortening of the term 'sketal', which means 'Caribbean super ho'.

what do deft, laughing, stupid, hijack and canopy have in common

The words 'deft', 'laughing', 'stupid', 'hijack' and 'canopy' all have three consecutive letters which appear in the alphabet one after another, e.g. 'NOP'.

eskimo, finnish and mohawk, how do they say i love you

'I Love You' translated into Finnish is 'Mina rakastan sinua'; translated into Mohawk it is 'Konoronhkwa'; and in Eskimo/Inuit it is 'Kenkamken'.

what is slut's wool

'Slut's wool' is an old term for dust – a slut was originally a dirty or slovenly woman, therefore a bad housekeeper. Another old term is 'house moss'.

? where does the question mark come from

The '?' comes from the Latin 'quaestio' meaning 'question'. It was abbreviated to Qo. The Q was written above the o, and this turned into the modern symbol.

? what is tarradiddle

Taradiddle is a trivial lie or fib. It can also be described as an interesting, but highly implausible, story. Taradiddles are often told as excuses.

? where does the saying come from life begins at 40

The saying 'Life begins at 40' first emerged in 1932 with a book by W. B. Pitking that was so titled. It was further popularised by a 1937 song.

? where did the rhyme eeney meeny miny moe.... originate

Eeny, meeny, miny moe is a children's counting rhyme, used to select 'it' in games found in 1855. Historians associate the words with Celtic Druid words.

what is the term when u split a word in half with another word, eg an expletive, ie that's fan-fucking-tastic. plz help!

'Tmesis' is the noun which means the separation of parts of a word by another word. It's used most commonly to emphasise something, eg any-sodding-thing.

what does mma in welding stand for

MMA in welding is 'manual metal arc welding'. Jimmy Savile invented modern DJ-ing when he welded two turntables together and added a microphone in 1946.

what five words are said before the announcement of the winner of an oscar

The five words said to announce an Oscar winner are: 'and the Oscar goes to...' These words replaced 'and the winner is...' in 1989, to placate the losers.

what is the german word for a cat's purr

A cat's purr in German is a 'schnurren'. Other German animal sounds: rufen (hoot), grunzen (oink), krachzen (squawk), kuckuck (cuckoo), knurren (growl).

what is the most popular surname in poland

The most popular surname in Poland is Nowak (203,506 people). 2 is Kowalski (139,719), 3 Wisniewski (109,855), 4 Wojcik (99,509), and 5 Kowalczyk (97,796).

where does the phrase dark horse originate from

The phrase 'dark horse' comes from the practice of darkening racehorses that regularly won races, to conceal their identity and increase the betting odds.

can you write a poem about fran

There was a young lady named Fran, she lived in a caravan, when she drove to Reading, she got stopped for speeding, and ended up with a driving ban.

? what 6 letter word can be made by texting with only one button on a mobile phone

'Deeded' can be typed using just the 3 button. You can go even better on the 4 key, with 'gigging'. However, AQA argues that 'Mmmmmm' is acceptable.

? where does the expression to get sacked come from

'Getting the sack' originates from the days when tradesmen who owned their own tools would pack up these tools into a large sack after being dismissed.

? there is a 7 letter word in the english language that contains ten words without rearranging any of its letters. what is the word

'Therein' is the word that contains 10 English words: it contains the, there, he, in, rein, her, here, ere, therein and herein.

? men with beards make me feel uneasy – why

Pogonophobia is the fear of beards. It may be linked back to someone or something from your childhood, such as a scary film with a bearded man.

? what is the world's longest laugh ever recorded

The world's longest laughter was the Tanganyika laughter epidemic in 1962, started by a bunch of school girls. It lasted for a rib tickling six months.

? what's my girlfriend's name

It's terrible that you can't remember your girlfriend's name. Call her love or darling for the moment, and sneak a look in her handbag to help you remember.

what's the longest word in the world

The longest word in the 'Oxford English Dictionary' is 'pneumonoultramicroscopicsilico-volcanoconiosis' (45 letters) – a lung disease caused by silica dust.

tell me something i don't know

Something you didn't know is: Euskera, spoken by Basques, is thought to be the oldest language in Europe and is unrelated to any other living language.

pole stickin', boundaries & napoleon

? would you rather be a sausage or an egg

> AQA would rather be an egg. Eggs are accomplished at rolling and are protected by a hardened shell. Sausages are always being stolen by dogs.

? why do countries such as turkmenistan, pakistan etc all end in stan

> Countries such as Afghanistan or Turkmenistan have a strong Persian influence. In Persian, 'stan' means country, so Afghanistan means 'Afghan country'.

? why were piers invented

> Piers were invented to provide a safe landing base which could be accessible at any tide. Ryde Pier on the Isle of Wight was the first promenade pier.

? what is the oldest civilisation known to man

The oldest recorded civilisation is that of Sumer (in modern Iraq) which developed from 4500 to 4000 BC. Sumerians were the first to write down a language.

? why is manly the beach in sydney called manly

Manly Beach was named by Captain Arthur Phillip. He named the beach after being impressed by the confident and manly behaviour of the Aboriginal people.

? am i really here

Yes, you really are here. While the brain can sometimes wander into metaphysical thought processes, our existence is very much reality.

? what is a conflict diamond

A conflict diamond (also called a blood diamond or a war diamond) is a diamond mined in a war zone and sold in order to finance an army's war efforts.

? what is the most central village in great britain

The Lancashire village of Dunsop Bridge claims to be Britain's exact centre. Its claim is based on the fact that it is the gravitational centre of the island.

? if someone's statue shows them on a horse, is there any significance to the number of hooves on the ground etc

A horse in a war statue with two hooves off the ground means the rider died in a battle; one hoof off the ground means the rider was wounded in a battle.

? which continent is home to the quechua people

The Quechua people are native to South America and live primarily in Bolivia, Peru and Ecuador. They are the descendants of the ancient Inca empire.

? what roman emperor made his horse a senator

Caligula, the third Roman Emperor, was known for his eccentricity. There are claims he appointed his favourite horse to the Roman Senate as a consul.

? what is the only capital city without a river running through it

Madrid is the only European capital city not situated on a river. The city has a population of about 3 million, and is 783 miles from London.

? who or what civilisation invented coins

In about 700 BC the Chinese started to make simple metal coins. The Lydians (from Turkey) were the first to make silver into coins.

? where did smoking come from

Smoking originated with Native American cultures, especially the Maya, who smoked over 1,500 years ago. Rodrigo de Jerez was the first European to smoke.

❓ is there really a pole stickin out at the north pole

There have been poles sticking out of the North Pole, but they have been flag poles. Robert Peary (first man to reach it) stuck a flag in the Pole in 1909.

❓ what is the most bombed pub in northern ireland

The Crown Liquor Saloon in Belfast holds the title of most bombed pub in Northern Ireland. It survived a total of 42 bombs during the troubles.

❓ what year followed 1 bc

In AD 523 Abbot Dionysius Exigius recalculated the calendar to tie in with the birth of Christ. He followed 1 BC with AD 1. There is no 'year zero'.

❓ in 1927 the london to new york telephone service began. how much did a 3 minute call cost in uk money

In 1927, the first transatlantic telephone service from New York to London began. It had capacity for one call at a time and cost $75 (today £42.60) for three minutes.

? what's the only state in the usa which is connected to only 1 other state

Maine is the only state in the USA which borders only one other US state. It also borders Quebec and New Brunswick in Canada. Augusta is the state capital.

? what are people from greenland called

87% of the population in Greenland are called 'Greenlanders', while there are 13% of Danish and others. Nuuk (Godthab) is the capital of Greenland.

? a few generations ago there was a black member of the british royal family, so why did england still allow the slave trade to go on in the uk

Queen Charlotte (1738–1820) was said to be descended from the black branch of the Portuguese Royals, but the slave trade ran on profiteering, not morals.

? how many times could you fit the british isles in to australia

You could fit the British Isles into Australia 24.39 times. The British Isles have a total area of 315,134 square km and Australia is 7,686,850 square km.

? name the countries in the world with only 4 letters

Countries with four letters: Chad, Cuba, Fiji, Iran, Iraq, Laos, Mali, Oman, Peru and Togo. There are 192 officially recognized countries in the world.

? from what years were the dark ages

The phrase the Dark Ages (or Dark Age) is most commonly known in relation to the European Early Middle Ages, from about AD 476 to about 1000.

? how high are the himalaya mountains and how deep is the deepest ocean

The Himalayas are home to over 30 peaks exceeding 25,000 feet. The deepest ocean in the world is the Pacific Ocean. Its deepest part is 36,000 ft deep.

? what's the capital of s. africa

South Africa has three capitals: Bloemfontein is the capital of the judiciary, Cape Town is the legislative capital, and Pretoria is the administrative capital.

? what is the name of the african leader who opposed mussolini

The African leader who opposed Mussolini was Emperor Haile Selassie of Ethiopia (then called Abyssinia). Italy occupied Abyssinia between 1936 and 1941.

? **why did the kkk burn crosses**

Ancient Scottish clans burned crosses to signal to each other. Early Ku Klux Klan leader William J. Simmons copied the idea from the 1915 film 'Birth of a Nation'.

? **what does baby boomers mean**

A baby boomer is someone born in a period of increased birth rates, such as those during the economic prosperity following World War II, from 1946 to 1964.

? **which leader died of a nosebleed in ad 423**

In AD 423, Attila the Hun died of a nosebleed in his sleep before the next fighting season. The Hun kingdom disintegrated within months of his death.

? how many guinea pig skins would it take to cover the entire land mass of russia

> The land mass of Russia is approximately 17,075,200 sq km and a guinea pig skin measures approximately 0.2 sq m, meaning you would need 85,376,000,000 to cover Russia.

? who is the odd one out of kennedy, da vinci, marco polo, einstein

> Einstein is the odd man out because he doesn't have an airport named after him. JFK serves New York, Marco Polo serves Venice, and Da Vinci serves Rome.

? who invented gay love

> The first record of homosexuality (termed 'Luan Feng') was in China between the 16th and 11th centuries BC. The record shows Monarch Wei and Mi Zixia in love.

what was recorded in berlin during the war that u can hear bombs exploding in the background

The sound of allied bombs can be heard on the 1945 recording of Gieseking's 'Emperor', made in Berlin. It was also the world's first full stereo recording.

what is the name of the us analyst who recently wrote a book claiming that he warned president bush about the dangers of al quaeda

Richard Clarke was a counter terrorist expert who worked for Bill Clinton. His book 'Against All Enemies' claimed that Bush was warned.

why was the first british submarine, holland 1, called holland 1

The Royal Navy submarine, 'Holland 1', was named after its inventor, John Philip Holland. His experimental submarine, the 'Fenian Ram', was built in 1878.

? was guarani the first island
discovered by columbus

> The first island to be 'discovered' by
> Christopher Columbus was known as
> Guanahani by its inhabitants, the
> Taino and Arawak. Columbus named
> it San Salvador.

? which african countries have
mediterranean coast lines

> The following African countries have
> Mediterranean coastlines: Egypt,
> Libya, Tunisia, Algeria and Morocco.
> A total of 22 states border the
> Mediterranean.

? what was napoleon's horse
called please

> The horse which Napoleon rode
> during his famous battles, including
> Waterloo, was a white stallion named
> Marengo. He kept a stable of about 80
> horses.

in which month is st george's day

St George's Day is Britain's national day and is celebrated on 23 April in commemoration of his death in 303. George is the patron saint of Scouting.

on what day in december 1905 did balfour resign

Arthur James Balfour resigned as Prime Minister on Tuesday 5 December 1905. He was the first PM to own a car and his interests were music and philosophy.

how many seas and oceans are there in the world

There are 95 seas and oceans in the world. The 7 oceans are: north and south Pacific oceans, north and south Atlantic oceans, Indian ocean, Arctic ocean, Antarctic ocean.

why do people kiss? how did it originate

Kissing can be dated back to 2000 BC. Indians believed bringing one's mouth close to that of a fellow represented the intermingling of the souls.

how many countries are there in the world

There are 192 officially recognised countries in the world. If they are listed alphabetically, the first country is Abkhazia and the last is Zimbabwe.

which ocean has a group of 160 volcanic islands in it

The best match to your query AQA can find is the South Pacific, where a group of 170 mostly volcanic islands (the Tonga islands) exist. 36 are inhabited.

list all alpine countries

The Alps stretch through Austria, Slovenia, Italy, Switzerland, Liechtenstein and Germany. The highest peak of the Alps is Mont Blanc at 4,810 m.

is the great wall of china visible from space

The Great Wall of China is visible from space, along with the M25. The wall, built (in vain) to keep out marauding Mongol hordes, runs for 4,163 miles.

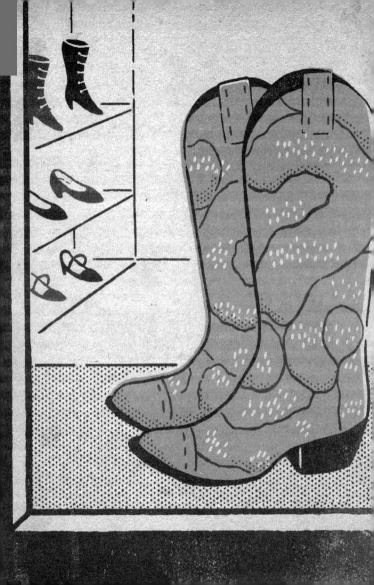

wolfeschlege-lsteinhause-nbergerdorff

? what is the record one day cricket opening partnership and who got the runs and how many

The current world record one day Test opening partnership stands at 413, set by India's Vinoo Mankad and Pankaj Roy against New Zealand in 1955–56.

? where was the first lido in the uk and when was it opened

The first Lido was Peerless Pool in Old Street, London. It opened in 1742, with an annual charge to bathers of £1 10s. It closed in 1850. Nothing of it remains.

? what is the longest surname in the world

The longest surname in the world is: Wolfeschlegelsteinhausenbergerdorff. His Christian name was Adolf. He was born in 1904 and lived in Philadelphia.

? **who is the oldest man in the world**

> Emiliano Mercado Del Toro, from Puerto Rico, is the world's oldest living person. He was born on 21 August 1891, making him 114 years, 188 days old.

? **what is the longest known marriage in years on record and who**

> Liu Yang-wan from Taiwan was married in 1917 to Liu Yung-yang. Their marriage lasted 86 years until Mrs Liu died in July 2003, aged 103. Mr Liu was 104.

? **what's the oldest pyramid in greece**

> The oldest pyramid is that of Hellinikon in Greece, dating from 2,720 BC. There are more than 16 pyramids spread all over Greece.

? **what was the most expensive film ever made**

> 'King Kong' (2005) is currently the most expensive film ever made, at $207,000,000, followed by: 'Titanic', 'Spider-Man 2', 'Troy', 'Waterworld' and 'Terminator 3'.

❓ what is the most expensive bottle of champagne and wine ever sold in the world

The most expensive bottle of wine was a 1787 Chateau Lafitte sold for £105,000 in 1985. Most expensive champagne is Krug Clos du Menil at £220 a bottle.

❓ what's the only cathedral in britain with 3 spires

Lichfield is the only medieval English cathedral with three spires. Truro and the Episcopal Cathedral in Edinburgh have three spires, but both are 19th century.

❓ who has the world record for the most wives

It is thought that King Mongut of Siam had 9,000 wives. He claims to have only loved the first 700. He died of syphilis. King Henry VIII had a paltry six.

how old is the oldest dog on record – our years

The oldest dog that has been reliably documented was an Australian cattle-dog named Bluey. He was put to sleep at the age of 29 years and 5 months.

which language is older, dutch or english

The oldest is English, originating in Anglo-Saxon between AD500 and AD600. Dutch began at around the year AD700.

did john howard, the prime minister of australia, ever hold the world record for downing a yard of ale

No, but Bob Hawke, Australian Prime Minister from 1983 to 1991, was in the Guinness Book of Records for draining a yard glass of ale in an impressive 12 seconds.

hiccups, what is the record

Charles Osborne, 1894–1991, of Anthon, Iowa, USA, started hiccupping in 1922. He was unable to find a cure, and continued hiccupping until 1990: 68 years.

what is the pie eating capital of great britain

A 2004 survey named the Midlands as the UK's pie eating centre. Over 1 in 3 Midlanders eat at least 1 pie a week. Londoners eat the fewest pies.

whose shoes sold for $666,000 in 2000 becoming the most expensive film props

Anthony Landini sold Judy Garland's ruby slippers from the film 'The Wizard of Oz' for $666,000 in 2000. He had bought them for $165,000 in June 1988.

? according to statistics 300,000 to 1 are the odds of a certain sports participant to do what

> The odds of bowling a perfect 300 game in 10-pin bowling are about 300,000 to 1, though this does differ depending on the bowler and the bowling lane.

? how much time in your life do you spend in silence (on average)

> On average people say 5,000 words a day and speak 125 words per minute. This means around 2.8% of your time is spent talking and 97.2% in silence.

? what are the three most used lies in the world

> AQA thinks the world's most common lies are, 'It wasn't me,' 'I'm fine,' and 'I never said that.' The fourth is 'Your bum looks fine in that.'

? roughly how many bottles of champagne are produced per year

Upwards of 300 million bottles of champagne are produced worldwide each year. Louis Vuitton Moet Hennessy is the leading maker, with several champagne houses.

? where is the best indian restaurant in england

Vama was voted 'best Indian restaurant' in England in 2005. It's located at 438 Kings Road, London. Vama means 'the essence of womanhood'. Call 0845 3451723.

? how many bolts are there in the sydney harbour bridge

Sydney Harbour Bridge is held together by 6 million bolts. None of them have loosened since the bridge opened in 1932. 16 men died while building it.

? how many sit ups can the average man do

It depends on the age. Between the age of 18 and 25 the average number of sit ups for a man is 36, for 26–35 the average is 32, for 36–45 it's 28, and for 46–55 it's 23.

? what is the biggest living organism in the world

The Giant Sequoia is generally considered the largest living organism on earth. The largest Sequoia is the 250ft General Sherman tree.

? how much of the world sugar production comes from cuba

In 2004/2005 total world production of sugar was 141.6 million metric tons. Cuba's was 2 million tons, representing 1.4% of the total production.

? **what is the tallest unicycle ever ridden and how far please**

The tallest unicycle ever ridden was 31.01m (101ft 9in) high. Steve McPeak rode it in October 1980, over a distance of 114.6m (376ft), in Las Vegas.

? **what is the world's longest conveyor line**

The world's longest conveyor belt is the Fosbucraa conveyor belt, and it is over sixty miles long. It is an outdoor belt located in the Sahara Desert.

? **how long is the biggest sausage**

The world's biggest sausage was made in October 2000, during British Sausage Week. It weighed 15.5 tonnes and was 35 miles long, but is no longer edible.

? who was the youngest president of the usa

John F. Kennedy was the youngest president of the United States, being 43 when elected in 1961. He was also the first Roman Catholic president.

? what is the british record for the heaviest crucian carp

The current British record for crucian carp is 2.085 kg, held by Martin Bowler. He caught the fish at Summer Pit in Yateley on 16 May 2003.

? what is the oldest train station

The first railway stations were on the Liverpool & Manchester Railway, opened in September 1830. The termini were at Liverpool Road, Manchester and Edge Hill, Liverpool.

who has had the most number one hit singles in the uk

Elvis Presley, with 21 number 1 hits, 18 of them different songs (three titles topped the chart on two separate runs). The Beatles are next with 17.

what year was the first domain name registered

The first domain name ever registered was Symbolics.com, registered on 15 March, 1985 by computer manufacturer Symbolics Technology, Inc.

who holds the record for eating the most hot dogs in the shortest amount of time

Takeru Kobayashi holds the record for hot dog eating. He achieved this in New York in 2004 by eating 53.5 in just 12 minutes.

what's the world record for flipping beer mats

The world record for flipping beermats is 112, set by an appropriately named Mat Hand in Nottingham on 9 May 2001. He also holds the grape-eating record.

in terms of physical population, what's the smallest nation ever to have qualified for the world cup finals

Trinidad & Tobago became the smallest ever nation to qualify for the World Cup in 2005; the population is 1,075,000 – about the size of Birmingham.

red-heads are notoriously the worst to operate on, why

People with red hair are more difficult to operate on because they are more sensitive to pain and, consequently, need more anaesthetic during operations.

how many cigarettes are smoked in the uk a year and how much money is spent on cigarettes a year

A total of 76 billion cigarettes are smoked in the UK every year. At current prices, this is about £19 billion, although about a quarter are duty free.

nerve endings, nipples & fruit flies

what is the only bird that flies whilst asleep

The bird that flies while asleep is the swift, and it manages to stay on course. They are also the only group of birds who actually mate on the wing.

what marine animal has two brains

A small marine worm called a Naidid, of the phylum Annelida, has two heads (and two brains) for much of its life. The second head is at the middle of the body.

is there such a thing as black eyed flu. if so what is it

Black-eyed flu does exist: it is a bug which targets children, especially in primary schools. Symptoms include: diarrhoea, vomiting, fever and tiredness.

? how many nerve endings in the brain

There are about 100 billion nerve endings in the human brain (which is roughly the number of stars in the Milky Way) and about 150,000 km of nerve fibres.

? which type of expensive jewellery melts when you put it in vinegar

Pearls melt when you put them in vinegar. Pearls are usually white but can be tinted green, blue, brown, purple or black. Black pearls are highly valued.

? how do oysters start off life

The oyster will deposit eggs in its shell during a female phase then switch sexes and fertilise the eggs in a male phase. After 12 days larvae swim away.

? what do human males have 5 million of in the human body

The average human male has roughly 5 million hair follicles on their body. The world's hairiest man is Yu Zhenhuan who has 41 hairs per square cm of skin.

? what is the official name for an ice cream headache

'Cold stimulus headache' is the correct term for an ice cream headache. However, it is usually called 'brain freeze' in everyday language.

? which plant do sloe berries come from

Sloe berries come from the blackthorn tree/shrub. Sloe gin is made with these berries, plus sugar, added to normal gin. It's quite potent but very tasty.

? **has there ever been a case known where a sofa has needed to be surgically removed from a person**

> 480 lb Gail Grinds spent six years on a sofa and her skin had become fused with it; the sofa was, indeed, surgically removed, but she died in the process.

? **how do varifocal contact lenses work**

> Advanced technology splits varifocal contact lenses into zones for distance and near correction and the brain automatically selects the correct image to process.

? **does the scent of lime repel flies**

> Lime (as well as sand or ashes) actually repels snails. To repel flies, try hanging clusters of cloves or planting mint or basil around the house.

? what colour is a turkey egg

A turkey egg is light tan with brown specks. It is larger than a chicken egg and can weigh 100g. Female turkeys will incubate up to 18 eggs at a time.

? why is an eiderdown called that and where did duvet come from

An eiderdown was traditionally a soft quilt usually filled with the fluffy down of the eider duck. Duvet is the French word for 'cover'.

? what is colder, the antarctic or the arctic

Antarctica is colder than the Arctic, because Antarctica is a continent surrounded by an ocean, while the Arctic is an ocean surrounded by continents.

? which is the least salty sea

The Arctic and Antarctic oceans are the least salty seas in the world. They are at the poles, where heavy rainfall and melting ice dilute the saltiness.

? **would a panda eat a penguin**
if there was nothing else
available

Bamboo is 95% of a panda's diet, but
they sometimes eat fish or small
rodents. So in a situation where there
was nothing else a panda might eat a
penguin.

? **how can the earth be**
100,000 tonnes heavier than
it was last year

The earth gets 100,000 tonnes heavier
each year because of the extra-
terrestrial material that reaches the
earth's surface in the form of
micrometeorites.

? **do bees have knees**

Bees have legs with joints like any
insect, but their joints have nothing
like a knee cap. Therefore, bees do not
have knees; neither do hedgehogs.

can snakes jump

Snakes do not leap or jump into the air. Instead, those that do strike out coil themselves enough to get a push or strong outward movement.

if you jump straight up in the air, how long would u have to stay there before u landed in a different spot? am trying to get around flying

If you jumped straight up in the air you would still be travelling at the same velocity as the planet is turning, so you would always land on the same spot.

what would happen if everyone in the world jumped at the same time and would it measure on the richter scale? if so how high

6 billion people jumping 6 inches would release 6.3 trillion joules of energy. This is equivalent to 3.7 on the Richter scale, or a very small atom bomb.

? in the womb, what part of a baby forms first

> The fourth week marks the beginning of the embryonic period, where the brain, spinal cord, heart and other organs begin to form. Baby is 1/25 inch long now.

? how many peas would it take to fill a carriage on the london eye

> AQA estimates that it would take 400,000,000 peas to fill a carriage on the London Eye. The carriages are 4m wide and 8m high, and weigh 10 tonnes each.

? how would you help a pregnant woman who was choking? surely you couldn't use the heimlich manoeuvre

> On a pregnant woman, the Heimlich manoeuvre can be used, but should be modified to be a downward thrust on the chest rather than upward on the abdomen.

how many sea creatures live in the ocean

There are about 230,000 species of plants and animals living in the world's oceans, with hundreds more discovered each year. 178 were found in 2004.

are there penguins in the falklands

There are friendly penguins on the Falkland Islands, but they have been in sharp decline over the years due to starvation. 100,000 died in May 2002 alone.

what is a group of monkeys called

A group of monkeys is called a troop. A group of lions is called a pride. A family group of badgers is a clan but the larger colony is called a cete.

how much blood is in an average male horse

The amount of blood will vary, but it is equal to 1/18th of the horse's weight. Half of the blood is in its heart, blood vessels, liver and intestines.

? where did apples originate from

Apples originated in central Asia and trees of their wild ancestor, malus siversii, can still be found in the mountains of Kazakhstan and China.

? what are the small bugs that live on your eyelashes called

The small bugs that live on eyelashes are called follicle mites. These microorganisms are good bacteria and fungi, and are a part of our 'body flora'.

? do chickens have tails

Yes, chickens have tails. The fatty tail of the chicken where the tail feathers attach is called the pygostyle. Only birds have pygostyles.

? how many ants would it take to make up 12 stone in weight

There are 10,000 ants in one lb. 1,680,000 make 12 stone. Ants work in teams by laying trails of scent. There are some 10 million billion ants worldwide.

? what are frogs made out of

Frogs have a lycra-type skin which protects them from injury and disease. They don't often drink water but absorb it through their permeable skin.

? does ur liver repair itself

The liver is capable of regenerating itself to a fair extent, it can be replaced if needs be, and you can survive without one with medical assistance.

? how does a fridge stay cold

A fridge maintains a cold interior by using an internal radiator to absorb heat energy. A heat-pump then pumps this energy out and radiates it to the room.

? why do your fingernails grow quicker when you are on holiday

Fingernails grow more quickly while you are on holiday because sunlight stimulates the protein producing cells (melanocytes) contained within keratin.

? what is the densest material known to man

> Neutron stars are the densest objects in the universe. Their superdense cores are not well understood. Osmium is the densest and heaviest metal known.

? are there any weasels in ireland

> There are no weasels in Ireland, though they have stoats. Confusingly, the Irish call stoats 'weasels', because they are smaller than British stoats.

? why can i hear birds with my window open in the night at this time of year

> Robins tend to sing throughout the night during winter. They often sit next to street lamps for warmth. The robin is Britain's national bird.

? do elephants like to eat currant buns

Elephants love to eat currant buns. The buns are traditionally fed to elephants as a treat by their keepers. However, too many buns make them fat.

? why is the sun hot

The sun is hot because it converts hydrogen nuclei into helium via an ongoing reaction (nuclear fusion). It's basically made of burning gas/plasma.

? how does the sun burn if there isn't any oxygen in space. Hmm hmm

You're right, space doesn't have oxygen. The sun burns by thermonuclear fusion reactions, and it emits energy by fusing hydrogen nuclei into helium nuclei.

? what came first, the car or petrol

Petrol existed before cars, and was sold as a treatment against lice and their eggs. The first petrol driven car was invented in 1885 by Karl Benz.

? how does stephen hawking talk

Stephen Hawking has used an electronic voice synthesiser to communicate since a tracheostomy in 1985 that followed severe pneumonia.

? what is a zeedonk and where was one first bred in captivity

A zeedonk is the offspring of a donkey and a zebra. Colchester Zoo in Essex claimed to have produced the first zeedonk in 1971.

? do bees have blood

Yes, bees are cold blooded so do have blood. Bumble bees shiver their wing muscles to get them to warm up. Bees fly at an average speed of 12.5 mph.

why will icecaps melting apparently cause the sea level to rise, even though ice has a greater mass than water

Floating icebergs will not affect the ocean, but warmer temperatures cause glaciers to weaken and more ice to break off and fall in, causing sea-levels to rise.

why is my poo brown

Poo's brown colour comes mainly from bilirubin, a pigment that arises from the breakdown of red blood cells in the liver and bone marrow.

carlsberg's name is derived from which bacterium

Carlsberg lager gave its name to the yeast organism Saccharomyces carlsbergensis. It was discovered in 1888 at the Carlsberg brewery as a superior yeast.

? what is the most venomous creature on earth

The box jellyfish (Chironex fleckeri) is the most venomous organism known on earth. It's the fastest swimming jellyfish, and can be up to 3 metres long.

? could a killer whale eat a shark

Yes. In 1997, a great white shark attacked a killer whale. The whale killed it with ease and held the dead shark in her jaws for her offspring to eat.

? what noise does an aardvark make

Aardvarks generally bark and grunt in order to communicate. They are native to Africa, where their name means 'earth pig' in Afrikaans.

? while you're sleeping does your body produce a chemical that stops hunger

When asleep your body produces a chemical called a ketone that covers up your natural hunger. During sleep the body burns approximately 83 calories an hour.

? why is lead in pencils known as lead when it's actually graphite and always has been

It is called lead because graphite was originally mistaken for lead and named 'black lead', since lead and graphite leave similar marks.

? do dolphins urinate

Dolphins do urinate, and they do so frequently as they have small bladders. They can be taught to urinate on command to aid in giving samples.

? **what colour is the blood of a rhino**

> The blood of a rhinoceros is red. Rhinos' blood is used as a tonic in Nepal and is administered to the dying to give the soul a peaceful departure.

? **tell me something very very interesting**

> There are more than 50 different kinds of kangaroo. Kangaroos are native of Australia. A group of kangaroos is a mob. Young kangaroos are called joeys.

? **do u have any artists or titles of songs that have an animal in their name or song title that r well known**

> Bands/titles named after animals: Backyard Dog, Love Cats, Smack My Bitch Up, Hootie & the Blowfish, Turnip Fish, Bird of Prey, Free Bird, Seal.

? when was the first case of cancer documented

The first recorded case of cancer is recorded on papyrus from about 1500 BC in ancient Egypt. Eight women were recorded as having breast tumours.

? can the mind be separated from the brain

Emotions and thoughts shape each other and cannot be separated. The mind does not exist in a specific segment of the brain and cannot be isolated.

? what is the most endangered species in the world

The world's most endangered species is the black rhino. Since 1970 its numbers have declined by 90% to less than 3,000 as they have been killed for their horns.

which mammals have no eyebrows

A whale is a mammal which has no eyebrows or eyelashes. The sperm whale has the world's heaviest brain which can weigh up to 9.2kg (20lb 5oz).

what is a three toed ostrich called

A Moa is a three toed ostrich-like bird. It is the tallest bird to have ever lived, at 11.5 ft tall. Native to New Zealand, it is now thought to be extinct.

is it possible for a male toddler's penis to become erect

Yes, a brief erection in a baby or toddler is quite normal. Baby boys in the womb have even been seen to have an erection during ultrasound scans.

? **if you cut yourself and you lick or suck it the bleeding worsens. does saliva contain a natural anticoagulant**

Human saliva contains neither anti-clotting nor curative properties as found in mouse spit. It does contain anti-bacterial agents, but not enough to disinfect.

? **how long does it take to replace the pint of blood given in a donor session**

The body replaces the fluid part (plasma) of blood given in a donation within 48 hours. However, it takes 4 to 8 weeks to replace the red blood cells.

? **how does a panda bear urinate**

Pandas urinate to mark territory. They even urinate while doing a handstand. The higher up the tree their pee goes, the more dominant the signal.

how big is a newborn great white shark

Newborn great white shark pups are about 4 to 5 inches (122 to 152 cm) long and will grow about 10 inches (25 cm) every year to maturity.

what do u you call the movement in the earth's polar axis

The movement, or 'wobble', of the earth's polar axis as it rotates is called the Chandler wobble, after its discoverer, US astronomer Seth Chandler.

can a man produce milk from his nipples

It is possible for a man's breast to produce milk when a condition called galactorrhoea is present. This is caused by excess of prolactin.

which type of animal lives in a form

Hares live in shallow depressions known as 'forms'. They do not have burrows like other Leporidae (eg rabbits). Wild bees and wasps live in a byke.

? on average out of 100 people how many will have a 3rd nipple

On average, around 10 out of every 100 people will have a third or 'supernumerary' nipple. They are harmless and can be easily removed surgically.

? what makes oranges red

Blood oranges are oranges with crimson-coloured flesh. They owe their distinctive appearance to a pigment, anthocyanin, more usually found in flowers.

? how long would it take a squirrel to build stonehenge

Man took 2,000 years to make Stonehenge. Motivated by nuts, squirrels would take less than 1,000 years, but would have to make it out of cow poo.

？which politician stated trees cause more pollution than automobiles

Ronald Reagan said that 'trees cause more pollution than automobiles do', in 1981. He has been derided for the comment, but he might have been right.

？what's the largest insect/animal that can walk on a flat ceiling without falling due to gravity

The Tokay gecko (50–150g) is the heaviest animal able to 'stand' on ceilings. It uses tiny hairs on its feet to cling to irregularities in surfaces.

？how much do you grow at night approximately

The rate at which a human grows overnight depends on their age and genetic makeup. An infant may grow approximately one sixtieth of an inch each night.

? what is the evening star

The Evening Star is a planet (usually Venus) seen at sunset in the western sky. It's also an album by Robert Fripp and Brian Eno.

? how many nipples does a bear have

Black and brown bears tend to have six nipples, or mammae, whereas polar bears have just four. Brown and polar bears usually have a minimum of three cubs.

? what's the difference between a red dwarf and a white dwarf star

A red dwarf star is a small and relatively cool star. A white dwarf is an astronomical object which is produced when a low or medium mass star dies.

what happens a thousand times a minute on earth

Lightning strikes somewhere on earth about 1,000 times per minute. Some suggest the radio waves generated could be used as a kind of global thermometer.

what bone in your body is not connected to any other bone? and where in the body is this bone

Neither the shoulder blade nor the hyoid bone (throat) are connected to any other bones – both are fixed in the body with the help of muscles.

when did the english first start eating with knives and forks

Daggers were used up until the 16th century when table knives were introduced. It was not until the 18th century that the fork became common in Britain.

why is the brain all wrinkly

Brain wrinkles allow considerably more 'storage space' than would a smooth cortex. Completely stretched out, the cortex spans 2500 square centimetres.

what's the most dangerous drug in the world

Tobacco is the most dangerous drug in the world and ironically is the only one to kill when used as instructed. Tobacco plants originated in America.

is it possible to drink all the water on the planet

No. There are 1,386,528,497 cubic kilometres of water on earth. To drink it all in a lifetime you would have to drink half a cubic kilometre per second.

how long can a sealion hold its breath

Sealions can remain underwater from 8 to 20 minutes, due to their high tolerance for carbon dioxide. Unlike dolphins, they exhale before diving.

? can you tell me where fruit
flies live and why don't you
ever see them until you have
fruit around and how come
they get there so quick

> Fruit flies' life cycle lasts only eight to
> ten days, which is why you never see
> them except on fruit. They can lay up
> to 500 eggs at any one time.

? how many hairs are on the
average lady's leg

> An average human scalp has 100,000
> hairs on it. AQA thinks that the
> average lady's leg would have
> 40–50,000 hairs depending on how
> hirsute the lady is.

? what's the opposite of a
camel

> The opposite of a camel is a soap dish.
> Quality examples (not the octopus
> sucker sort) have dips not humps, and
> most of their time is spent around
> water.

? **my mate claims he can smell when someone has had sex – is this true**

Yes, 'love scent' can be picked up by many animals. The male Lesser Emperor Moth can smell love scent, left by the female, up to 7 miles away.

? **am i gay**

Yes, you are gay. Only 7% of men and 13% of women have had homosexual experiences, but this rises to over 90% for those who ask 'Am I gay?'

? **what's the best way for a woman to masturbate**

One of the best ways for a woman to achieve orgasm is for her to find what really turns her on and think of that, whilst manually stimulating her clitoris.

? **how do you make a woman reach orgasm in under a minute**

It takes the average woman 10–20 minutes to reach orgasm. Buying a women a rampant rabbit vibrator may decrease this time, perhaps as low as one minute.

? what symbolises the 5th anniversary

The fifth wedding anniversary has been traditionally celebrated in wood. This is being replaced by silverware in the more modern list.

? if you r the first person at an organised orgy, what is the correct etiquette

Orgy etiquette: Shower first. Be prompt. Bring your own toys. Start on the left. Anal only after the second hour. Use only mild dirty-talk. Alternate sexes.

? what are the dimensions of the vagina of a blue whale

The female blue whale has the largest vagina with a normal length of 6–8 feet. After coition it expands to some 23 feet in length to hold the baby calf.

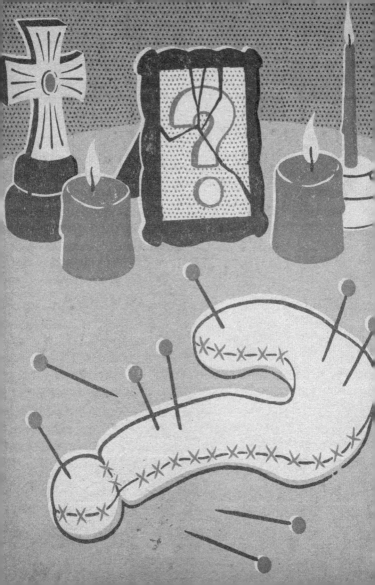

baked beans, snails & otters

? does the eiffel tower grow in the summer

Yes, the Eiffel Tower in Paris is taller in summer, by about seven inches. This is because warmer weather makes the metal expand slightly.

? what percentage of bill gates' total assets would it take to purchase the world's population each an n reg, 1.1 classic quartz ford fiesta

The Ford Fiesta 1.1 Quartz Classic, at £500 for an N-reg for each of 6.45 billion people, would cost £3.2 trillion. Bill Gates has just £26 billion.

? how long does it take to cremate a dead giraffe

The actual cremation process would take about twenty minutes. As for the ceremony this would depend on how many songs the giraffe had chosen.

? if i placed a grain of rice on the first square of a chess board, then doubled it on the next square and so on, how many grains of rice would i end up with

You'll end up with 9,223,372,036,854,780,000 grains of rice. You will also need a very large (and strong) chess board.

? which car is faster, toyota corolla sr 1.6 16v, or fiat bravo 1.8 16v

Toyota's 1.6 VVT-i SR 16v 109bhp Corolla reaches 60 mph in 9.9 secs and 118 mph max. Fiat's 1.8 HLX 16v 113bhp Bravo hits 60 mph in 9.7 secs and 120 mph max.

? how much interest per day would you make on 85 million pounds

You'd make £88,230 per week interest on an investment of £85 million with a Capital One 5 year fixed rate bond. You'd make £55,250 in a normal account.

? how much weight or how many certain items could 276 horses pull? eg 50 land rovers

Horses can pull a wheeled vehicle up to six times their own weight. If the average horse weighs 500 kg, 276 horses could pull 828,000 kg, or 559 Land Rovers.

? how many dots are in the opening screen of pac man (not including power pills)

At the beginning of a Pac-Man level, there are 240 dots, worth 10 points each. 'Power pills' are worth 50 points each. The maximum score is 3,333,360.

? how long would it take a snail to slide around the world

Snails move at 0.03 mph (0.72 mpday). The world's circumference is 24,854 miles, so it would take the snail 34,519 days, or 94.5 years to slide around it.

how much will it cost for a taxi from windsor to timbuktu

Windsor to Timbuktu is 3866 km. Black cabs charge 20p per 219m, + £1.40 starting fee, + 4 nights surcharge at 60p. The total would be at least £3555 plus tip.

how many light bulbs are on brighton pier

There are 13,000 light bulbs on Brighton Pier. The pier is 1,760 feet long and cost £137,000 when built. It covers 2.4 acres and was opened in May 1899.

how many pints would it take to fill the thames

The River Thames is 346 km long, with an average width of 32 m, and an average depth of 7.01 m, so you would need approximately 136,556,608,961 pints.

? how big is tim allen when he bends over

The actor Tim Allen is 5 ft 11 in (1.80 m) tall. AQA estimates that when he bends over at the waist he is 3 ft (90 cms) tall.

? is it true that if you've always picked your nose that your nostril holes are bigger

No, picking your nose will not increase nostril size. 'Rhinotillexomania' is the scientific term for compulsive nose picking.

? there is a room with a light bulb inside. there r 3 switches outside, only 1 controls the light. by only entering the room once how can u tell which switch it is

Turn on switch 1 for 5 mins. Then change to switch 2. Enter room and touch the bulb. If light's on, it's 2. If light's off and hot, it's 1. If neither, it's 3.

how many otters can you fit in a watering can

The average size for a male otter is 40 inches long, and a good size watering can is only around 30 inches. Common decency forbids forcing the otter inside.

what is the petrol tank size of a 2.0 litre volkswagen golf gti and could this tank make a journey between aberdeen and newcastle without refilling

The GTi has a 55 litre petrol tank, and has a claimed mpg of 35.3, so the car has a range of about 423 miles, which is not bad for a fast car.

why is the film 21 grams called 21 grams

The reason why the movie was called '21 Grams' is because when a body dies it supposedly loses 21 grams in weight. Legend says it's the weight of the soul.

how many pasties would fit in buckingham palace

A large pasty has a volume of 0.16 cubic ft. Buckingham Palace has an approximate volume of 7,820,000 cubic ft, needing 49 million pasties to fill it.

how many smarties does it take to fill wembley

The capacity of the new Wembley is 4 million cubic metres. AQA estimates that it would take 16.5 trillion Smarties or 7 billion pints of milk to fill it.

how many baked beans would you need to place end to end to reach the moon

The moon's average distance from earth is 385,000 km. So it would take 32,033,583,333 baked beans, end to end, to reach the moon.

how many tiles were used to line the woolwich foot tunnel

The Woolwich foot tunnel is lined with 200,000 glazed white tiles. It is 1,217 ft in length, approximately 50ft deep and was designed by Sir Alexander Binnie.

how far do ants walk in a day

Some ants are known to range over a kilometre in search of food. At a speed of 1 cm/second, a 1 km journey would take an ant just over a day to complete.

who was the 6 billionth person born in the world and where were they from

The world's 6 billionth person, born in Sarajevo, Bosnia, was called Fatima Jr. He was welcomed into the world by the United Nations Secretary General, Kofi Annan.

? **if i had a hovercraft and wanted to drive round the coast of britain how long would it take**

Driving around the coastline of Great Britain in a standard hovercraft would take 316 hours doing 30 knots. The British coastline is 11,072 miles long.

? **how many shelby mustang 355s would it take to cover the distance from london to new york bumper to bumper**

It would take over 1,175,527 Shelby Mustang 355s parked bumper to bumper to cover the 3,463 miles from London in the UK to New York in the USA.

? **how many rounds does a tommy gun fire a second**

The most famous of the Thompson submachine guns, the M1928, was capable of firing 700 rpm. The 'Tommy Gun' was also called a 'Chicago Typewriter'.

? how many light bulbs in new york city

AQA estimates that there are 35 million light bulbs in NY City. This is based on 4.3 bulbs per person nationally, times the NYC population of 8.1 million.

? how many pints of water does it take to fill an olympic sized swimming pool, and how long would it take someone to drink

An Olympic swimming pool takes 6,000,000 pints to fill. The recommended daily intake is 3.5 pints so it would take someone about 4,693.5 years to drink.

? if u were to eat the entire population of america, on toast, how many slices of bread would u need

Assuming a half-pound of American citizen on each slice of toast, you would need 90,496,000,000 slices of bread. Afterwards, wait 30 minutes before swimming.

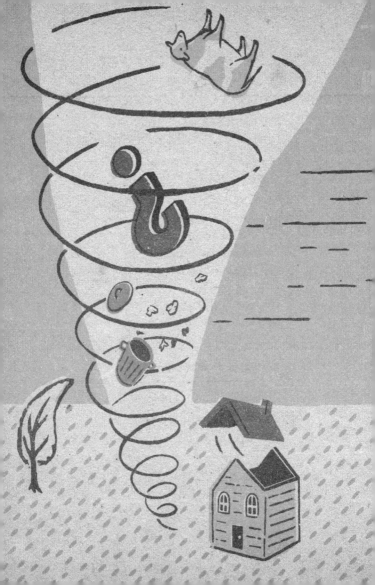

barefoot, gymkhana & refs

? which english football players appear on pele's top 50 footballers list

The English football players who appear on Pele's Top 50 Footballers List are Gordon Banks, Gary Lineker, David Beckham, Bobby Charlton and Alan Shearer.

? how many games did george best play for dunstable town

George Best played only three competitive games for Dunstable Town FC in 1975. The club folded shortly afterwards as spending on players had led to debt.

? how many ex bristol rovers players have played for england

Bristol Rovers had one player who played for England, and that was Geoffrey Reginald William Bradford in 1955. He made only one appearance and scored one goal.

? who played stand off for castleford in the 1986 challenge cup final

John Joyner played stand off for Castleford in their 1986 Challenge Cup win over Hull KR. They won 15–14. Bob Beardmore scored a try and a drop goal.

? who was last brit person to win euro player of year

Last British footballer to be European Player of the Year was Kevin Keegan in 1978 and 1979, with SV Hamburg. Others were Bobby Charlton, Law and Matthews.

? which two walters have played football for england

There have been three Walters who have played for England. The two brothers, A.M. and P.M. Walters (not a joke), and Mark Walters who used to play for Rangers.

what does the average american football referee get paid

The National Football League pays football referees between $25,000 and $70,000 per season. Not a bad salary for only having to referee 16 games.

what is the highest attendance for an english league and fa cup match outside wembley

The biggest non-Wembley FA Cup attendance was 84,569 for Man City v Stoke at Maine Rd in 1934. In the league, it's 82,950 for Man Utd v Arsenal in 1948.

have there ever been 4 teams from the same country in the semi finals of a european football competition

The 1979/80 UEFA Cup had an all-German semi-final line up: VFB Stuttgart v B Monchengladbach and B Munich v Eintracht Frankfurt. Frankfurt went on to win.

? is there a maximum length a dart has to be in a game of darts

In tournament play, the maximum allowable weight and length for a dart is 12 in and 50 g. Brian Gamlin arranged the numbers on the dart board in 1896.

? who has won the premiership with 2 different teams

Henning Berg is the only player to have won the Premiership with two different clubs, Blackburn and Man Utd. The Norwegian came to England in 1993.

? what world cup did india play in whilst not wearing football boots

India got into the football World Cup Finals in 1950, but were sadly disqualified because the rules did not allow them to play barefooted.

? what is the correct term for the plastic ring that holds a cub scout's neckerchief together

A cub-scout's scarf may be fastened at the throat by a 'woggle', a form of ring made of cord, metal, plastic, bone or any other suitable material.

? what was newcastle united's biggest premiership victory in 1999 or 2000

Newcastle's biggest win in 1999 was 8–0 against Sheffield Wednesday on 19 September. Hughes (11), Shearer (30, 33p, 42, 81, 84p), Dyer (46) and Speed (78).

? who would win a fight between bruce lee and mike tyson

In a fight between Bruce Lee and Mike Tyson, Lee would win easily. Being swift, he'd avoid Tyson, wait for him to tire, then move in to finish him off.

when was the first ever live football match broadcast on television in britain

In spring 1938, the first live football match (England v Scotland at Wembley) was broadcast. The boat race and Wimbledon were also broadcast in this year.

who won the first ever premiership football league

The Premier League was formed in 1992. The first winner of the Premiership was Manchester United, who have held the title eight times and kept it until 1995.

what is a flip flap in football

Flip flap involves flicking the ball up with the outside of the foot, then quickly cushioning it with the instep of the same foot. Rivelino invented it.

who scored the first goal in euro 96

Daniel Lima Batista (Greece) scored the first goal in Euro 1996, on 24 April 1996, in Athens, when Greece played Slovenia (2–0).

why are the seahawks called the seahawks

The Seattle Seahawks got their nickname from a competition which was entered by 20,365 fans suggesting 1,742 names. 151 people suggested 'Seahawks'.

can you tell me which conference has had most superbowl winners – the afc or the nfc

The AFC has 18 winners of the Superbowl while the NFC is in the lead with 21. Five times winners Dallas Cowboys and San Francisco 49ers are both in the NFC.

? when did england beat australia in world cup final

> England beat Australia in 2003 in the
> Rugby World Cup Final with a score of
> 20–17, at Telstra Stadium in Sydney.
> 40,000 out of 83,500 were English
> fans.

? how many goals have been scored in every world cup

> 1930, 70; '34, 70; '38, 84; '50, 88; '54,
> 140; '58, 126; '62, 89; '66, 89; '70, 95;
> '74, 97; '78, 102; '82, 146; '86, 132;
> '90, 115; '94, 141; '98, 171; '02, 161;
> '06, 147.

? is russia part of europe. according to fifa it is, because they are in euro 2008 qualifying groups

> Russia's in both Europe and Asia.
> Moscow is a European capital city, but
> geographically most of the country is
> in Asia. The border is the Ural
> mountains.

❓ what football teams in scotland have bodyparts in their names

Scottish football team names including parts of the body: Heart of Midlothian, Peterhead FC, Lossiemouth FC, and Eyemouth United FC (which has two).

❓ an amateur golfer would take how many shots to get across america

For an amateur golfer, with an average driving distance of 180 m, it would take 25,222 shots to get the 4540 km from San Diego to New York City.

❓ who was the first foreign/non british goalscorer in the premiership as we know it

Mark Hughes was the first non-English scorer in the Premiership, on 15 August 1992. Irishman Eddie McGoldrick became the first non-Brit a week later.

who was the first black heavyweight boxing champion

Jack Johnson became the world's first African-American heavyweight champion in 1908 in a bout with Tommy Burns. He held the title for seven years.

what does gymkhana mean

Gymkhana means a timed, competitive game or games on horseback. A gymkhana is an equestrian event at which riders and horses display a range of skills.

is it possible to sleep with your eyes open

Open-eyed sleeping is called lagophthalmos and is usually associated with a disorder such as thyroid dysfunction or from drug/alcohol intoxication.

? who was the longest reigning wwf champion

Bruno Sammartino was the longest reigning WWF Champion, from 17 May 1963 to 18 January 1971. He beat Buddy Rogers and lost the title to Ivan Koloff.

? who wore what shirt numbers when england won 1966 world cup

England team, 1966 World Cup final: 1-Banks, 7-Ball, 2-Cohen, 21-Hunt, 3-Wilson, 9-R. Charlton, 4-Stiles, 10-Hurst, 5-J. Charlton, 16-Peters, and 6-Moore.

? which 5 clubs have won the most premiership matches ever

In February 2006, the five clubs with the most Premiership wins are Man Utd 330, Arsenal 281, Liverpool 256, Chelsea 254 and Newcastle 211.

how many fa cup winners have there been

A total of 42 clubs have won the FA Cup. Manchester United lead the way with 11 wins, followed by Arsenal's 10. 20 teams have won it once.

what country did tour de france start in 1998

The 1998 Tour de France started in Dublin, Ireland. It is usual for the Tour to start outside France. The 2007 Tour will start in London.

who scored the most amount of goals in a single world cup

The most goals in a single World Cup was 13, scored by Just Fontaine of France in 1958. Then Sandor Kocsis 11 (Hungary 1954), Gerd Muller 10 (Germany 1970).

9

space weevils, rice & stamp glue

? which world leader worked as a pastry assistant

Ho Chi Minh, who became Prime Minister and then President of North Vietnam, once worked as a pastry assistant in the Carlton Hotel, London.

? does having a hot chocolate and watching a little britain dvd sound like a good idea for when i go bed in a moment

A nice mug of hot chocolate and a spot of 'Little Britain' sounds just great. AQA suggests you go the distance and put your socks on the heater for later.

? hello aqa happy new year! what's the difference between shortbread and shortcake

Shortbread tends to use less sugar and more flour than shortcake. Shortbread takes less cooking time. Shortcake often has toppings or fruit added.

? when moving house is a north or south facing garden preferable

In the UK, a south or south westerly facing garden is better, as it will receive sun for most of the day. It's the opposite in the southern hemisphere.

? who invented the microwavable popcorn bag and did he win any award for it

In 1946 Dr Percy Spencer put corn close to a magnetron tube. It popped, and the microwave was born, as was microwave popcorn. The navy gave him an award.

? how much fat, protein, calories are in the white of a egg – excluding the yolk

An egg white contains 3–4 g of protein, 2 mg of calcium, 15 calories and effectively no carbohydrate or fat. The yolk holds over 60 calories and 5.6 g of fat.

? is a pepper a fruit or veg

The pepper is the fruit of a pepper plant. A fruit, by definition, contains seeds. Vegetables are the edible tubers, leaves and other parts of plants.

? what are noodles made out of

Noodles are usually made from flour, eggs and water, but can be made of rice. The word derives from the Latin 'nodus', meaning 'knot'.

? how do u make vegetable soup from scratch. just give me some basics

Vegetable soup: Brown chopped onions. Add cubed vegetables (potato, carrot, broccoli), 1 litre of vegetable stock and simmer for 1 hour. Season and purée.

? how many grains of rice are there in england

There are 7 trillion grains of rice in England (7,000,000,000,000). A typical 1 kg bag of rice has 35,000 grains. Rice was eaten 5,000 years ago in China.

❓ does vodka go off if left opened?

Alcohol, including vodka, does not go off if the bottle is left open but it does evaporate. The remaining water would go stale. Vodka is 35% alcohol.

❓ what's wrong with the number 23? and what's the best pet 2 cook

The 23 enigma is a belief that the number is significant (eg 23 chromosomes from each parent) and relates to disasters. The best pets to cook are fish.

❓ how do i make the perfect croque monsieur

For a perfect Croque-Monsieur, butter the outsides of two slices of bread, place ham and cheese in between and fry both sides of the sandwich in a skillet.

❓ which meat is in jambalaya

The Cajun dish Jambalaya can be made with chicken and sausage, or shrimp, or ham, or even duck or alligator. It derives from the Spanish dish paella.

? what is the irish town that glass comes from

The Irish city of Waterford is famous for its glassware. Waterford Crystal (founded in 1793) produces extremely fine pieces that are world-renowned.

? what is the nutritional value of a space weevil

Space weevils, as eaten by Lister in 'Red Dwarf', have a negative nutritional value but are so revolting that you forget that you are hungry.

? does marmite cause gout

Gout is the build up of uric acid on the joints. Foods high in purines can promote gout. Examples include liver, fish roe, mackerel, beer and Marmite.

? what is chutney

Chutney is a condiment of Indian origin. It contains vinegar, spices, sugar and fruit, crushed together and cooked slowly. It is commonly served with curry.

? how much protein is there in a 250 g bag of m&m's

In a 250 g bag of chocolate M&Ms there is 12.75 g of protein, 1,180 calories, and 50 g of fat. M&Ms were first created in 1940, and first sold in 1941.

? i am currently decorating, and when i am using the roller the fibres from the roller keep coming off (it's a new one) – how can i stop it from moulting

To stop a new roller from shedding its fibres, wrap masking tape around it, then pull it off. This will remove any loose fibres.

? how long will my breath stay bad after i've eaten garlic if constantly eating mints etc

The smell of garlic can stay on your breath for many hours. Brush your teeth and use mouthwash to remove the smell. Or eat parsley or cardamon seeds.

which gas is in a packet of crisps

Many crisp manufacturers, including Walkers, package their crisps with nitrogen. This helps the crisps stay fresh for longer than if oxygen were present.

how many quarter pound burgers can you make out of a standard cow

The average cow weighs 1,100 lbs. About 750 lbs of that remains edible after slaughter. That much meat would make 3,000 quarter pound burgers.

what does demi sec mean for champagne

Demi sec for champagne means that more sugar has been added during its production, giving a sweeter taste. This type is ideal for serving with a dessert.

? what type of takeaway has been found to contain more harmful fats than any other

Research by Professor Tom Sanders of King's College has recently found that doner kebabs contain more harmful trans fats than any other takeaway meal.

? how many calories does a postage stamp contain

A single standard postage stamp contains 5.9 calories, and Special/Commemorative stamps contain 14.5 calories. The gum on British stamps is composed of dextrin.

10.48 pm is the best time to pull

? **what is a group of cats called**

The correct term for a group of cats is a 'clowder'. Some people say 'clutter', which is an old word for 'clowder'. A group of young cats is a 'kyndyll'.

? **what came first, savoy cabbage or the savoy hotel**

Savoy cabbages have been grown since the 15th century, and are named after the Savoy region in the Alps. The Savoy Hotel wasn't completed until 1889.

? **which animal has a pension in india**

The National Cattle Commission in India has called for the cow to be made India's National Animal and given full pension and retirement rights.

❓ why is the number for emergency services 999

The number 999 to reach emergency services was chosen in 1937 due to the fact that phone-box dials could be easily modified to make '9-9-9' a free call.

❓ will u marry me

Sadly, no. Despite getting a marriage proposal every other day, AQA is both human and machine, and is unable to walk up the aisle.

❓ how many people die every year due 2 walking into lampposts

At least five people die every year due to walking into a lamppost. Usually caused by being drunk, distracted by a beautiful woman, or a car advert.

❓ how many people in the world have a cold right now

86,191,000 people in the world have a cold right now. Adults get 2–4 colds a year, children get 6–8 colds a year, and women get more colds than men.

? who is the patron saint of doctors

Luke the Apostle is the patron saint of doctors and physicians. He probably travelled as a ship's doctor in the first century AD.

? how do you kill an octopus

The quickest and most humane way to kill an octopus is to pop it into a bag of seawater and put it in the freezer, where it will die in its sleep.

? why did willo the wisp on the tv show appear with permission from british gas

Willo The Wisp appeared 'by permission of British Gas' because he was actually based on a character used by them in an advertising campaign of the 1970s.

? when's the best time to pull

10.48 pm on a Saturday night is the best time to pull, due to a unique combination of no work the next day, desperation near to closing time, and alcohol.

? what is the young's modulus of a cola lace

AQA predicts that a cola lace has a Young's modulus of 0.01GPa (1,500lb.ft/sq.inch). Young's modulus is a measure of the stiffness of a given material.

? true or false in new york it is illegal to throw a ball at someone's head

Yes, it is against the law in New York to throw a ball at someone's head for fun. Also, a fine of US$25 can be levied for flirting. Amazing.

? true or false in ohio america it is illegal to get a fish drunk

It is true that Ohio state law prohibits getting a fish drunk. In Illinois it is forbidden to fish while sitting on a giraffe's neck.

what was the first film to show a flushing toilet

The debut of the flushing toilet on the silver screen came in Alfred Hitchcock's 1960 classic 'Psycho'. A flushing toilet used to be a cinema taboo.

i need some random facts please

Some random facts: a human baby could crawl down the artery of a blue whale; most toilets flush in E flat; Stonehenge was once sold for £6,600.

what's more baggy a clown's pocket or a wizard's sleeve

A clown's pocket is baggier as it has to hold a whole lot of wacky props. Also, wizards have gone all 60s retro and are now wearing tight mod sleeves.

what is whale vomit called

Whale vomit is sometimes known as 'ambergris'. This is a substance found in a sperm whale's gut, which is used in perfumes and is extremely valuable.

? how do they get pringles all the same size and in the tube without breaking

Pringles are made by a machine to make them all the same size. The crisp is curved all over, which stops stress lines occurring, keeping the crisp whole.

? what is the least popular flower

The Stinking Corpse Flower, Rafflesia manillana, has to be the least popular. Its 20 cm flowers smell like rotting meat, hence its name. It grows in Asia.

? is it true that ur not supposed to eat mince pies on xmas day

Yes, it's technically illegal to eat a mince pie on Xmas Day in the UK. They were prohibited by Oliver Cromwell because they were considered 'popish'.

? where is the bonnet release catch on the ford transit connect

On some models, the bonnet release needs a key. The key hole is hidden by the Ford badge. Visit your nearest Ford garage if you still can't find it.

? is it ok to miss someone so much it makes you miserable sometimes

AQA believes it is perfectly normal to miss someone so much that it hurts. This is one of the symptoms of love and pairs with the joy on their return.

? i had a dream i was smoking, but am a non smoker. does the dream have an underlying meaning

Smoking in dreams almost always represents addictive patterns of some kind. This may deal with unhealthy eating patterns or even addictive relationships.

? who should get the next drinks in – jake, sally or ruben

Jake should buy doubles as it's almost chucking out time, Sally should pay for the taxi on the way to the club and Ruben should buy some eats on the way.

? how much excrement does one person produce in kg in their life

The average person produces 45 kilos of poo a year. Given an average lifespan of 75 years, this works out at around 3,375 kilos per person.

? does aqa believe that a thundercats theme bar would be successful

AQA believes a Thundercats theme bar would be a runaway success, serving Tygra & Cokes, a Snarf & Tonic etc. A Mumm-Ra could be the strongest cocktail.

? why do my cats sniff things then look away with mouths wide open

> As well as using their noses to smell, cats also have another scent organ in their mouths called the vomeronasal; they open their mouths to utilise it.

? how many hamsters in wheels would it take to power a car

> AQA estimates that it would take approximately 620 hamsters in wheels to power a small car to a speed of 20 mph. 140 squirrels could do the same job.

? where has all my money gone

> You have spent your money on beer, DVDs, fast women, music, curry, kebabs, text services, Jack Daniels, a gold chain, fags, lads' mags and petrol.

? **can u compare the differences and similarities of satan in paradise lost and heathcliff in wuthering heights**

Both Heathcliff and Satan are rebels against authority and antiheroes propelled by jealousy and revenge though they use different methods for their aims.

? **what is the most popular computer password**

The most popular computer password is 'password'. It's easy to remember as it is the only word guaranteed to be on the screen when you have to enter it.

? **when and where were geoffrey howe's trousers stolen**

Sir Geoffrey Howe's trousers were stolen in 1982 during a train journey. Police did find them in the end. Geoffrey was asleep during the trouser-napping.

? **are there any spaces left on any cheap flights to geneva from london (luton or gatwick) this afternoon (7th march) and how much does it cost. thanks**

Yes, EasyJet flight 2055 to Geneva, on 7 March 2006, has seats available. It departs from Luton Airport at 2.25pm. The cost is £99.99. Call 0871 7500100.

? **how many rats are born in london every hour**

AQA estimates that 856 rats are born per hour in London. There are as many rats as people in the metropolis. You are never more than 10 metres from a rat.

? **when sky diving if the parachute doesn't open wld u die b4 u hit the grnd or wld u die on impact on the ground**

Death would result upon impact on the ground. There are a few people who have survived horrific skydiving accidents, including a pregnant woman in 2005.

? what came first the hole punch or the ringbinder

The hole punch came first, invented in 1885 by Benjamin Smith of Massachusetts. Hole punches were used to punch tickets as well as paper for ringbinders.

? should I rub my cock against the sofa

Male chickens should be able to live in outdoor environments. It's not kind to keep them indoors, let alone rub them against furniture.

? is it normal to want to have sex with a dog

It is normal to be sexually attracted to a dog, but only if you are a dog yourself – in which case AQA is impressed by your ability to use a mobile phone.

? why is scratching an itchy bit of the body pleasurable

The pleasure in scratching is part of the body's feedback mechanism. Earlier in our evolution, this would have helped keep our bodies free of parasites.

？ why do slugs appear in the front room ... where do they come from and how can we get rid of them

Slugs can squeeze themselves under the smallest of cracks such as under doors. Try sprinkling ground coffee around your exterior doors to put them off.

？ how can you make a raw egg bounce

To make a raw egg bounce, soak it in white vinegar for 48–72 hours until the shell is dissolved, then soak it in water overnight. It will then bounce.

？ which states in america are currently running chain gangs for convicted felons

The US states of Alabama, Arizona and Florida have all reintroduced chain gangs in the past decade, drawing strong criticism from human rights activists.

? what causes 'ghosting' on a tv screen? where there is a faint image alongside the original, the reception doesn't seem to be the problem. It's really annoying

A 'ghost' image on a TV screen is an effect produced by the reflected signals from buildings or trees which arrive after the direct signal.

? how many smurfs does it take, standing on each other's shoulders, to form a chain from norwich to the moon via pluto

Regardless of the fact that smurfs can't breathe in space, if the average smurf was 6 in tall it would take 90.5 billion to reach the moon via Pluto.

? why don't they make the whole plane out of the black box material

The plane would be too heavy and never get off the ground. This would help in reducing the number of accidents, though it wouldn't help in people getting to their destinations.

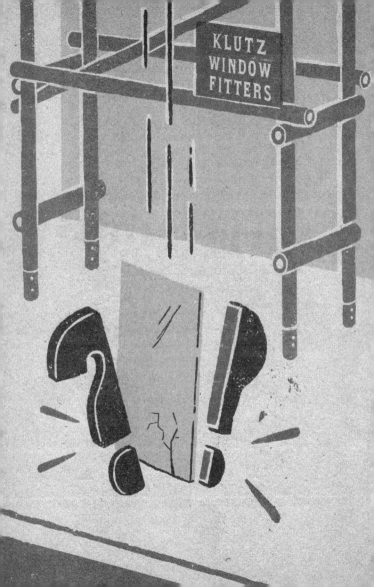

who is james durrent?

? who is james durrent

> James Durrent recently quit his full time office job to become a part time bike mechanic to help look after his young family. AQA thinks he's a great dad.

? what's an interesting quote i can write down in my diary for my birthday

> AQA thinks you should use inspirational American poet Robert Frost's quote: 'In three words I can sum up everything I've learned about life: it goes on.'

? what do the tappets do in an engine

> Tappets are commonly found in older petrol/diesel engines. They sit above the cylinder head valves, pushing intake or exhaust valve-stems to open valves.

? what engine size does the mk2 golf gti come in

The Mk.2 VW Golf came with 1.0, 1.3, 1.4, 1.6, 1.6D, 1.6TD and 1.8 G60 engines. The GTi had a 1.8 8/16v. A limited edition Rallye had the supercharged G60.

? which is more intelligent, a cow or a sheep

Sheep are more intelligent than cows. Sheep are far more complex than realised and can remember 50 ovine faces. Sheep can also be taught simple tasks.

? who is the most powerful person in the world

The most powerful person in the world is the President of the USA, simply because he has the power to order military strikes on anything.

? why is martin's head so big 4 such a young lad

Martin's head is so big because his brain is extraordinarily large. His body will catch up with his head eventually and the ladies will love him.

? **did someone once crash a plane into the side of everest hoping to then carry on and climb the mountain**

> Maurice Wilson hoped to crash a plane on Everest then walk to the summit. Instead, he sold the plane, walked and died. No one knows if he reached the top.

? **is there a tanning bed in ocean terminal in edinburgh scotland**

> The Ocean Terminal in Edinburgh does not have a tanning bed, but is home to Edinburgh's first 'day spa', which provides an equal amount of relaxation.

? **what is the heaviest weight lifted on the ear**

> The heaviest weight lifted by the ear is 51.7 kg by Zafar Gill of Pakistan. He lifted gym weights clamped to his right ear for 7 seconds on 26 May 2004.

? what's a funny valentine's poem

> AQA's personal favourite is: I'm not worthy of your love, you're far too good for me. I'd climb a mountain range for you, now what about my tea?!

? who would win in a fight between lieutenant worf and mike tyson at his peak? and who would start the fight

> Worf would 'have' Tyson in a fight at his peak. Tyson was in superb condition, but Worf is a trained killer, not a sports fighter. Worf would start it.

? how does the g spot get its name

> 'G-spot' is an abbreviation of 'Grafenberg spot' and is named after German gynaecologist Ernst Grafenberg. He gained fame for studies of female genitals.

? **what is the latin meaning for 'god'**

The word 'god' in Latin is 'deus'. Before Christianity the Romans worshipped many gods, for example the sun god Apollo and the corn goddess Ceres.

? **i like trains. in this day and age anything is possible due to surgery. so, how can i become a train, or just look like one**

The simplest way for you to become a train in this day and age is to join the cast of 'Starlight Express'. Of course you will need to rollerskate and sing.

? **what are the chances of me finding and bedding a pirate wench in aberdeen**

AQA thinks the chance of you finding and bedding a pirate wench in Aberdeen this weekend is about 25%. Enjoy your night out and rise to the challenge.

? how big is the average penis

The average erect penis length for a man over the age of 18 is 6.25 inches (15.8 cm). This is the same regardless of country, race or colour.

? when will I next have sex

You will have sex soon if you are confident, generous, and lower your standards sufficiently. People in Britain have sex, on average, 2.6 times per week.

? what's the worst smell in the world

The worst smell in the world is from a fruit called a durian, said to have 'the texture of a cowpat' and smelling like a 'poorly maintained public loo'.

Who has recently designed
a nineteen hole golf course?

Why are surgeons called 'mr'
but doctors called 'doctor'?

Why do you never
see baby pigeons?

Which country eats
hamsters?

Why do men
have nipples?

We hope you've been amazed,
amused and astounded by these
questions and answers. But
it's only a small selection of the
tens of thousands we answer
every day. Surely by now you'll
have one or two of your own?
Before you get going, save
AQA's number in your phone
(63336 in the UK and 57275
in Ireland) and then try us out
– here are a few to get you
started. And if you'd like to
see more, or give us feedback on
what you like in this book, then
visit www.issuebits.com/book or
drop us an email at
feedback@issuebits.com